Noel B. Jackson's,
The "B" is not for bald

Authored By

Noel B. Jackson
Shereena Morrow-Jackson

Illustrated By

Samuel Wilson

I am Noel B. Jackson Jr. and I have NO hair!
Have you ever got out the bed with no hair?

Me either! I didn't just wake up bald. At first, I woke up with one little patch all gone, just missing.

I didn't like that. It made me sad. How silly would I look with a patch of hair not there?

My Mom said, "You are still very handsome! Don't worry. It will grow back."

But that patch didn't grow back. Every day more and more hair fell out!

I was sad and then I was angry! Why me? Why did I have to be the only Kindergartener with no hair?

My Mom and Dad took me to the doctor. The doctor tried so many things. She gave me medicine to drink and then she gave me pills to swallow. None of that worked! I was still losing hair!

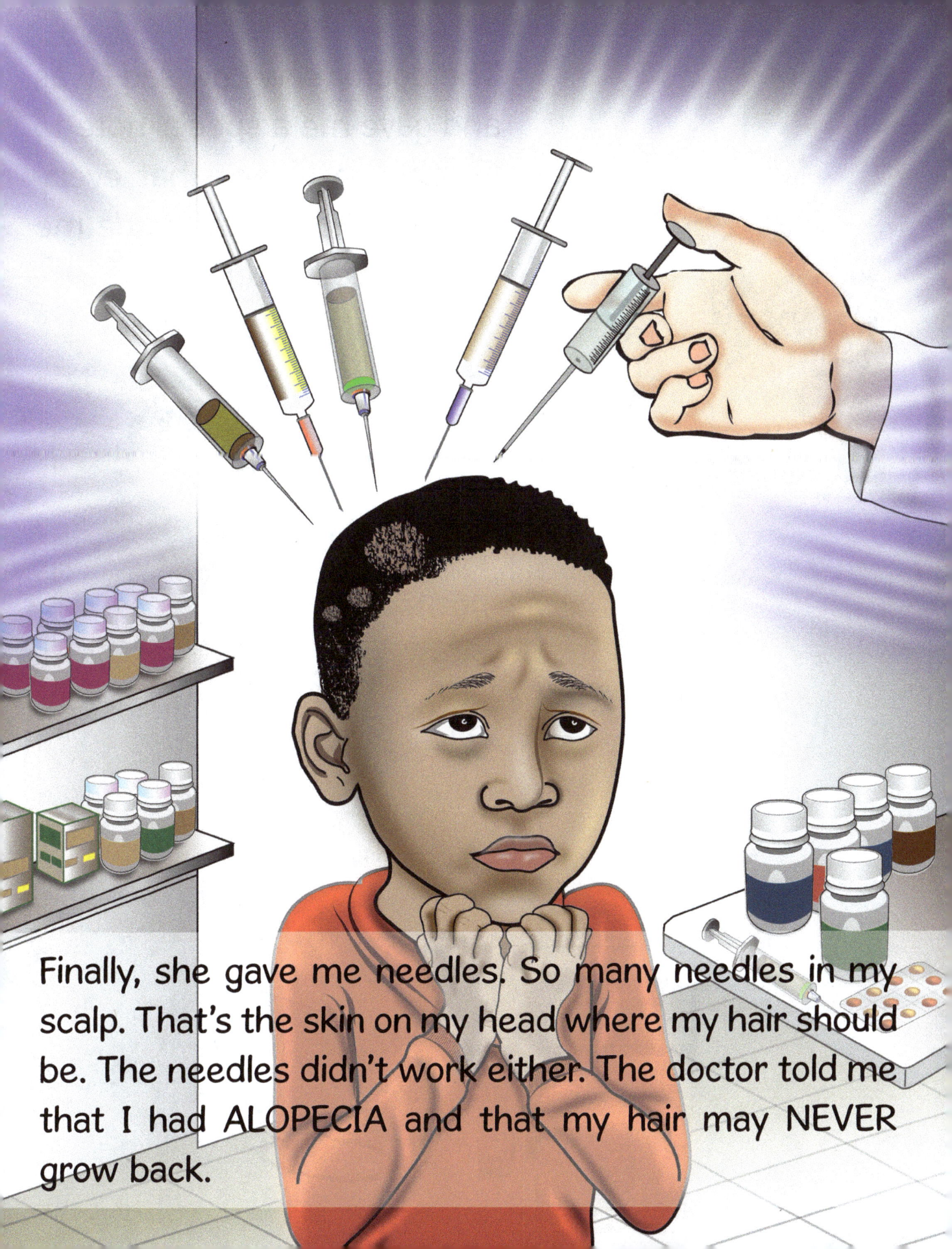

Finally, she gave me needles. So many needles in my scalp. That's the skin on my head where my hair should be. The needles didn't work either. The doctor told me that I had ALOPECIA and that my hair may NEVER grow back.

The doctor saw how sad I was and gave me a special note to be able to wear a hat every day to school. That made me feel a little better!

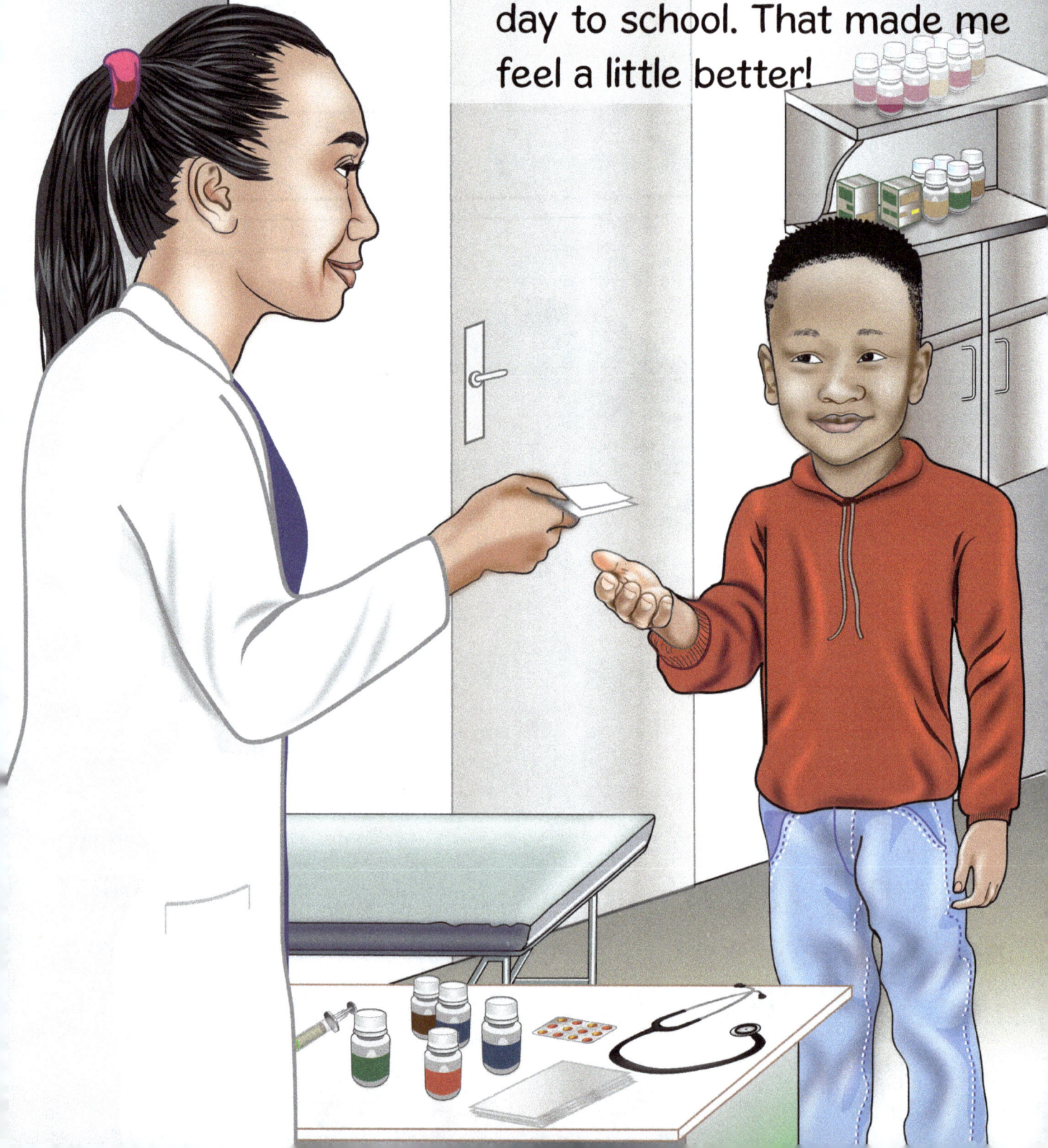

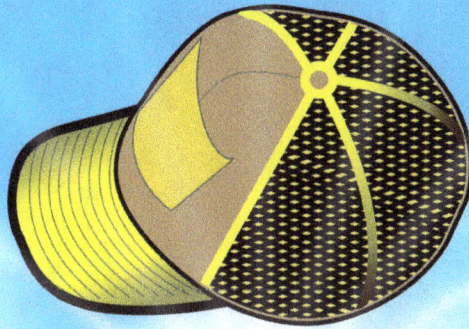

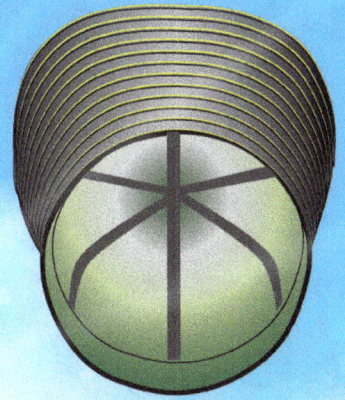

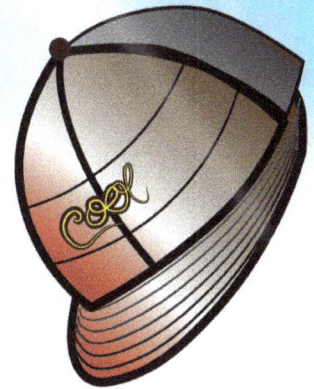

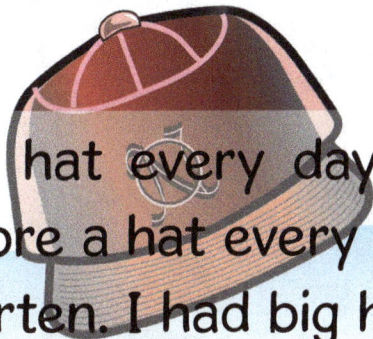

I wore a hat every day for the rest of the school year. I wore a hat every single day the summer after Kindergarten. I had big hats, little hats, and red hats. I had dressy hats and 17 baseball caps!

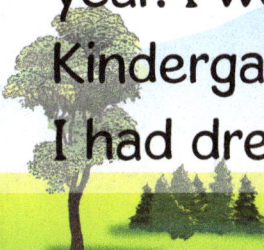

But even with all those cool hats, I was still sad and HOT!

I was sad because I had to hide myself every day. I was a little angry because I was super sweaty under all those hats.

One day, I decided that I didn't want to hide anymore. I wanted to go to first grade without a hat. I wanted to feel like me again.

So, I asked my Mom and Dad to cut the rest of my hair off. There really wasn't a lot left to cut.

My Mom was proud I was being so brave! My Dad was happy because he got to pretend to be a barber.

When the day came to get my hair cut, I was so nervous. I sat so still in my Dad's chair. I heard the clippers. Bzzzzzzz Bzzzzz.... Now, I was terrified!

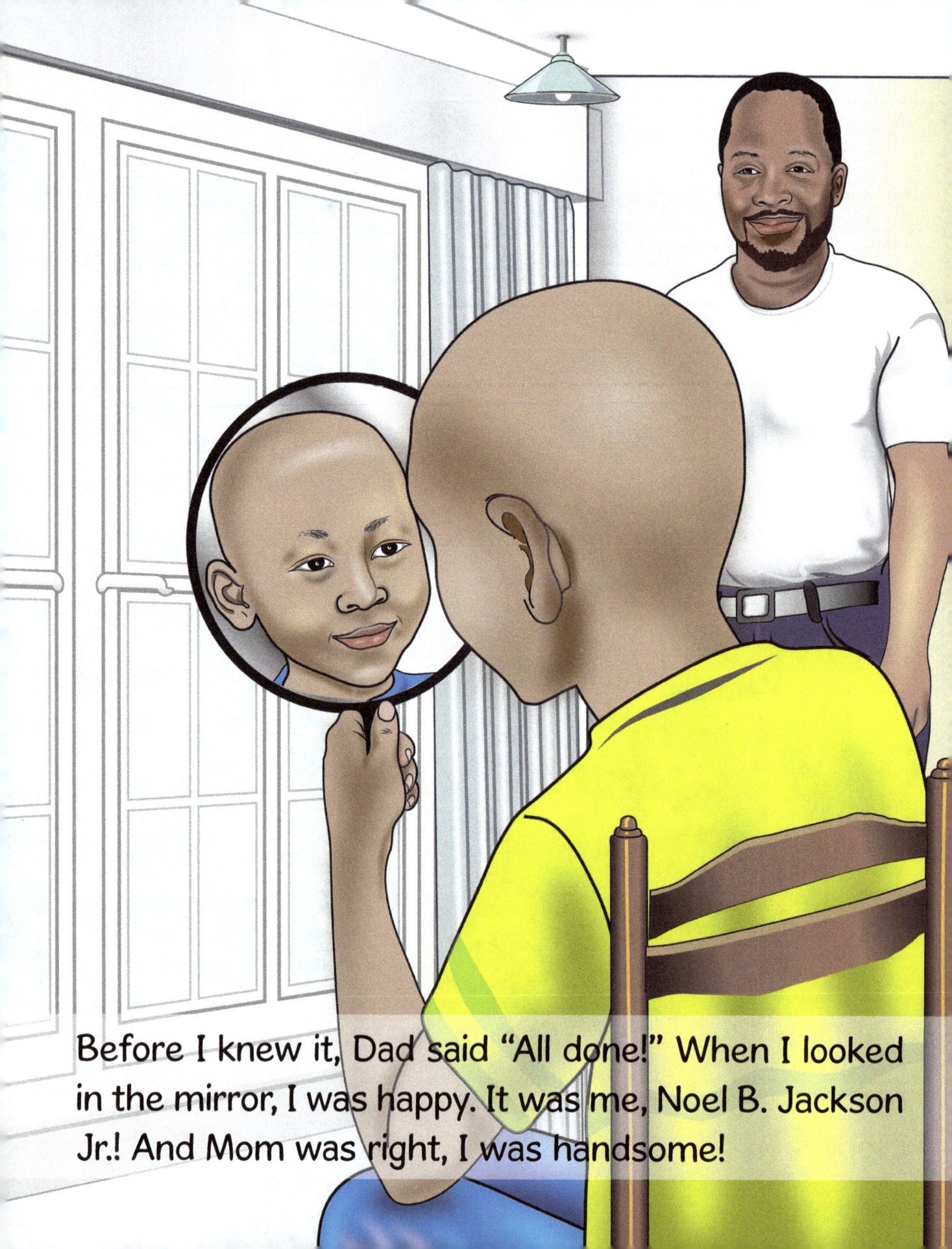

Before I knew it, Dad said "All done!" When I looked in the mirror, I was happy. It was me, Noel B. Jackson Jr.! And Mom was right, I was handsome!

I was ready for first grade!

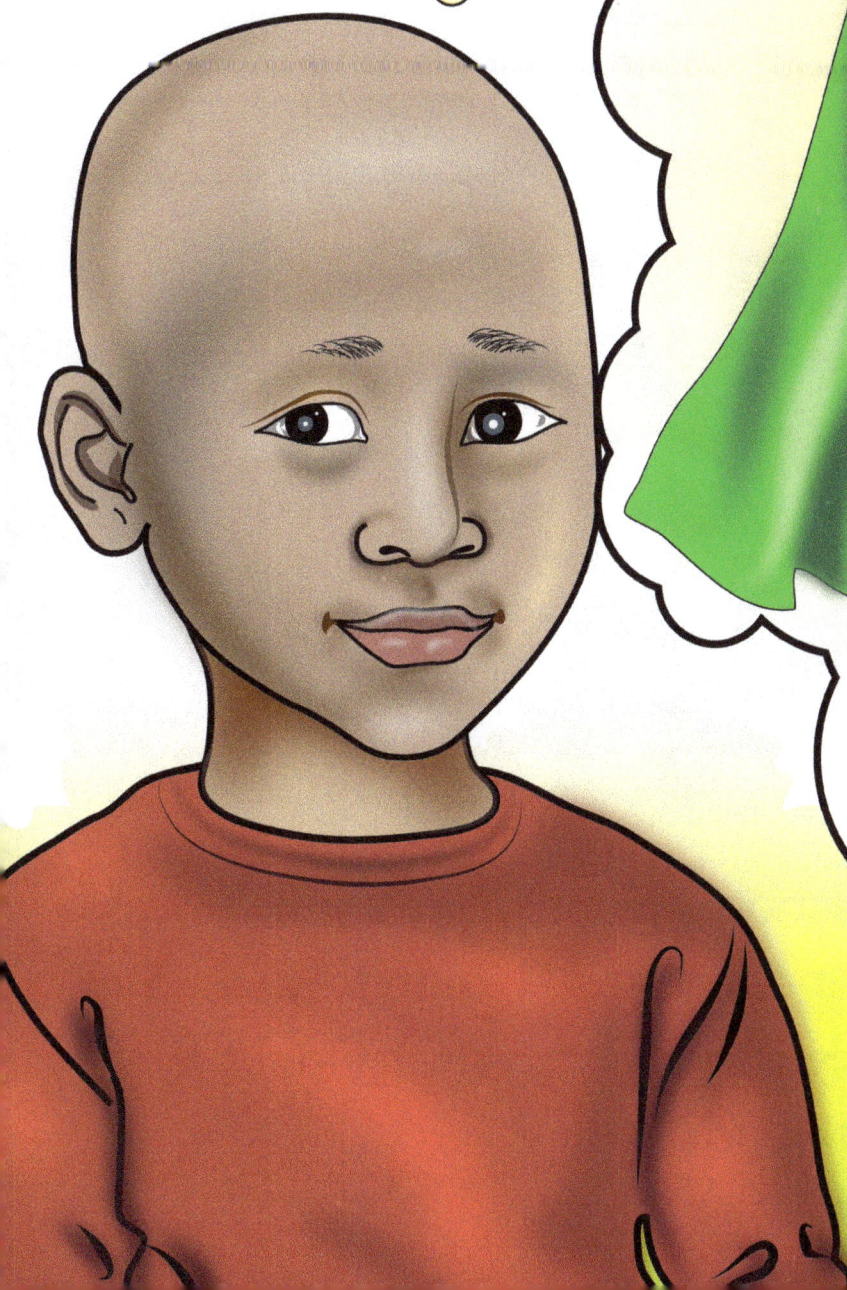

The night before school, I couldn't sleep. I was nervous about making friends. I didn't want the other kids to think I was weird. What would they think about my bald head?

When I got up for my first day of 1st grade, I felt confident. I felt like I was supposed to be bald. Yup, I definitely was suppose to be bald. It fit me.

But when I got to school, walking across the yard, I got a lot of stares. I started to feel sad but I remembered what my Mom told me. I remembered that I am special and even more handsome without hair.

So I took a deep breathe and held my bald head high. So high that I made eye contact with someone. She smiled and said "Hi, I'm Sarah."

I was excited on the inside. I couldn't believe it, my very first 1st grade friend.

I smiled back, "Hi, I am Noel Bartram Jackson Jr. and I have no hair."